Southern Breezes II

Rhymes, "Rahms," and Ravings of a Gentle Mind

William M. Finnin, Jr., Th. D.

The Marshpiper Press

Southern Breezes II: Rhymes, "Rahms," and Ravings of a Gentle Mind
ISBN: Softcover 978-1-946478-28-3
Copyright © 2017 by William M. Finnin, Jr.

All rights reserved. No part of this book may be reproduced or transmitted in any form or by any means, electronic or mechanical, including photocopying, recording, or by any information storage and retrieval system, without permission in writing from the publisher.

Cover Photograph of Morning on Atlantic Beach, Florida by William Finnin.

To order additional copies of this book, contact:

The Marshpiper Press
1-423-475-7308
www.parsonsporch.com

The Marshpiper Press is an imprint of **Parson's Porch & Book Publishers** in Cleveland, Tennessee, which has double focus. We focus on the needs of creative writers who need a professional publisher to get their work to market, **&** we also focus on the needs of others by sharing our profits with those who struggle in poverty to meet their basic needs of food, clothing, shelter and safety.

Southern Breezes II

Rhymes, "Rahms," and Ravings of a Gentle Mind

Memory

Divine dust angels' wings

    ground fine

        by time

Contents

By Way of Introduction 9

Foreword 13

Eucharist 15

Speculative Theology 16

The Net 17

Invincible Walls 19

The Poet's Knife 20

Last Train for Change 22

Little Things 23

Caffeine Poet 24

Sometimes 25

Alethea 26

Lonely Season 28

True Gifts 29

Madeira Tears 31

Ambivalence 32

Alone 34

Navel 35

The Source 36

Bold 37

Can You Imagine 38

Dazzled 39

A Story Poem 40

Scorched 42

Nightwalker 43

Bag Lady	44
Reaching	45
Three Words	46
Uncertain Courage	47
I Will Not Go	48
Proposal	49
A Body Considered	50
Milestones	53
Prayer-Poem for Graduation's Eve	54
Commencement Prayer	56
First Dance?	58
Moonlight Dances	59
Holy God, We Bow Before You	60
A Child's View … Prescience?	61

By Way of Introduction

"Spin me a "rahm,'" she wrote. And to this day, I can't say or think "rhyme" without flashing back to Catherine Williams' enchanting encouragement in 2003-2004 during a period of inspirited creativity and ecstatic imagination. While this little offering of "rahms" doesn't present many "rhymes," I hope it evokes a smile, a raised eyebrow, a quizzical rumination and perhaps even a long-lost experience or two. Poetry doesn't require rhyming to bring delight of spirit or dissonance of thought that conjures memory and meaning.

So take these "rahms' as you will. They are but an offering, created over time and out of the disorder and disarray of authentic living. The joy they seek to express as well as the pain to which they point are real. Take them to mean the meaning you alone must assign. Take them as mere snippets and snapshots of juxtapositions of personal thoughts and fleeting memories.

There are no over-arching themes or subtle organizational structures to be discerned from the sequence of these "rahms" and ramblings. Their creation spans several decades, the first written and actually published (in *Boys' Life*) more than six decades ago! Most found voice and pen in recent years.

To this day, despite serious work in the subtle nuance of poetic crafting under the thoughtful creative mind of Jack Myers, poet Laureate of Texas, teacher-friend at SMU, and the tender encouragement of my late-arriving personal muse, I am still intrigued by John Ciardi's question, posed five decades ago in his small but valued volume: *How Does a Poem Mean?* I am but a novice still trying to grasp this process without compromising the process itself. Doubtless, I was better at it then than today. Please pardon the kinks and knots and erstwhile gaps.

With the exception of two poems here reprinted, both autobiographical, *The Net (published in 2009)* and the final brief entry penned and published at the age of nine as a Cub Scout in

Clermont Harbor, Mississippi, few eyes have seen these offerings or heard these rahms read.

If there's meaning for you in any of these scribblings, you will have to tease it out and make that meaning your own. After all, that's the "meaning" of meaning! Isn't it? Or else it's meaning-less. So, pick and choose, skip or discard as you may be inclined. The writing's all mine but the choices are entirely yours.

If not too audacious, my hope is that you may discover yourself in at least one crafted thought that follows ... and then freely craft a few of your own.

William M. Finnin, Jr., Th. D.
Sebastian, Florida

2017

For two most precious and inspirited souls

Aaron Ladd Finnin

and

Helene Annie Finnin LaBourdette

My son the artist and my sister the horse-whisperer

Foreword

"Poetry is a mirror which makes beautiful that which is distorted."
— Percy Bysshe Shelley

William "Will" Finnin and I have been colleagues for almost twenty years. Before that, we came of age in the 1960s, those extraordinary years of civil rights struggles, new visions of social justice, greater inclusivity in government and institutional religion, and uncovering silenced voices, of women, Black and Hispanic Americans, and countless others throughout history. I honor him for his contributions in all of these areas.

But my regard for Will goes beyond our shared generational goals. Rather, it is more about his belief that the redemption of the human spirit is always possible in our uncertain world.

Will is an artist, and his talents are amazing. He is a musician, a painter, author, counselor, and more. But I believe that it is his poetry that has continued to sustain him and others for a lifetime. His poetry has given expression to the flow of his life in all of its moments of pain, joy, survival, uncertainty, and courage. His words are testaments to his vision of transformation.

Sylvia Plath wrote that mirrors "have no preconceptions," and that is why it takes such courage to look into them. As I have read Will's poetry over the years, I know that it emerges from a profound inner experience. I think of it as a world where he has dared to enter a house of mirrors that Plath speaks of, a place where their concave and convex images have given him a special understanding of what it means to be human. Will has dared to witness the power of these reflections to reveal the paradox of our lives. He has dared to enter that complex maze that shows us reality in infinite ways and makes us question our ordinary preconceptions. Like a haunting kaleidoscope, this world calls us to stretch our imagination. He understands that enlarging our imagination is crucial for us, both personally and collectively.

But more. Will has dared to return from this experience with vital new visions of renewal. He has experienced the fullness and fatefulness of life. He has known great joy. He has suffered great pain. But he continues to affirm life, and to seek beauty and regeneration through creativity. His writing speaks to us of lives shared, lives celebrated, lives wondrously known.

Through his art, he has striven to do what writer Jane Kenyon calls "the poet's job," to express "feelings we all have that are so deep, so important, and yet so difficult to name."

This is what poetry is all about, and this is how it saves us.

As a poet, Will understands this job, and he offers this volume from his serious yet playful heart, his life, and his vision of a joyfully transformative human spirit.

— Catherine Williams, Ph.D.

Eucharist

The bread is baked, hot warm.
Its rich-roast perfume inviting all to table
as from the oven it emerges.

Fresh flour ground raw and whole with oil and yeast combined
for kneading, rolling, pressing down
to rise into a loaf that brings both joy and health.

And health twice new this loaf affirms and offers fresh
the fragrance of the holy.
Broken it will be to heal old wounds of spirit, heart, and mind.

Broken with the broken here,
where nourishment is found and in the taking, eating,
healing memory mends both shattered hearts and souls.

Speculative Theology

God was

giddy

downloading creation

that night …

at least

an ironic smile.

God the trickster

shaped us each

from dust

so we'd come clean

with Her

fresh

forever

free

The Net

Dripping wet against his thigh it rests,
lead weights their circle drawn;
hoisted there a thousand times before
on mudflats shallow draught.

He casts his round, a circle full,
smooth sway to left then right again,
his teeth clenched loose around the sacrament,
the grey lead host.

His hands grasp nylon, fingers ready for release;
his wrist cinched tight
by line five lengths the net.

He spins and turns,
throws arms outstretched as if
in answer to that low-tide Neptune's call.

The net itself takes form and spreads seamless
its mosaic of fine nylon tugger lines and weights.
In blur of light it flies against dull brown of mud-filled bay.

He's had this net since he was once a child
when, nearly tall as he, they'd struggle through
the sand, wade in chest deep
and try to cast his spell.

In time he mastered throwing while the mullet fed;
developed stealth of stalking birds,
and filed his gunny sacks with bounty near the shore.

For years the net hung loose on nail pins in his shed,
mute memory of what used to be.
He'd grown away from marshes, beach, and sand.

But in his heart to mudflats he'd return,
and from its safe protected place retrieve the net,
secured with memories sweet
of endless walks on ebb tide flats
packed full with hungry fry just pleading to be caught.

Then he'd rest net on naked dripping thigh,
grasp hanks of nylon
lips around the lead,
and sway.

A dancer who alone can heed the beat:
full left while net swings smooth across his feet
then right again and up up up to meet rare air
to cast that spell which from the deep sends chill.

And once the net is loosed,
shapes nylon round,
he then retrieves all that swam 'neath his feet.

The net, once cast, has all but lost its spell.
He's older now and all his youth is spent.

The net, the mullet, shrimp, and little fry
swim free as memories on the falling tide.

The net, its tiny knots in place,
no breaks, no tattered cords,
sits bundled, boxed and safe.

But out on morning sandflat filled with happy fry
he casts a vision,
cleansing heart and marsh itself …

Invincible Walls

How small the human mind that builds its walls
    to keep new ideas out,
      blocks their ascent to consciousness.

A tragedy to live within that box,
    untutored by horizons stretched and unfamiliar
    where interests bear unsettling strangeness,
    threaten change.

Hermetic seals screen eyes from cultures broader than the brow,
    and generate fear to fend off curious spirits
    for risk-free safety's sake.

Should pity follow
    or courageous probes
      where sentient knowing shatters blissful ignorance?

The Poet's Knife

The poet's knife cuts flesh and gristle with equal ease,
    slices down to air-naked bone,
    eviscerates with one slow slash.

A wound to name and cleanse a wound, she writes,
    seeking that ancient poison sac,
    festering in seclusion's dark,
    concealed by time from memory,
    to lance it.

Her word-blade glistens red with life,
    self-cauterizing as it slides
    through constricted capillaries that feed
    malignancies deep unseen
    in privacy long-protected and preserved.

To heart of life she plunges,
    scalpel-sharp her blade,
    certain that to excise is to heal:
    in piercing health returns.

Sure and sharp her syllables bisect hurt,
    puncture worn assumptions
    where concealed shadow memories
    of past pains reside.

No longer safe and silent,
    they spring forth with pressured pulse,
    releasing putrefying pus of past mistakes,
    resentments and unprocessed angers
    hankering for forgiveness and new health.

Naming is her art which,
    when conjoined with skilled poetic craft,
    liberates wounded hearts grown weary-worn
    with the heavy loads of loss.

Horizons broaden with new-day's dawns
    as incremental hope returns
        to friendships broken and betrayed.

No longer festering in denial's silence,
    a wearied soul revives to live again.

Acceptance manifests the gracefulness of pain.

Last Train for Change

Sweet Suwannee silenced a poet's voice,
>shuffled him aside amid the clutter of what passed for real,
>consumed in daily trivia,
>rendered mute.

Sidetracked by palpable illusion.

Here in this place he did not choose, he sometimes thought,
>"I'm living someone else's past
>that has not future vision
>nor guilt for what's forgot."

A once-dear promise of creation
>broken by expedience and fear;
>a history frozen into institutions
>framed by tribal conflicts etched in stone.

Once-strong-now-frail connective threads stretch taut in panicked crises,
>gossip-nurtured and abetted by stale curiosity
>embedded in worn-out ways few understand
>but most have fought to save.

Time's consumed by self-absorbed adult children,
>whose scheming games dull focused thought,
>while reasoned judgment waits to catch
>the last train out of town.

Little Things

Funny, isn't it?

Those little things that make for memory,
        and form who we become.

The ones that seem so boring normal in the moment,
        obscured when first occurred,
        yet now forever fixed in mind.

Mysteries, they rotate, return:
        fulcrums of meaning,
        balance points of living oscillations,
        filled with memories' joys
        and tears.

Little things …

Caffeine Poet

"Some of my best creating I do in the air," he said.
And what happens when you come down,
   land, you know?" she asked.

"Well, if I can get to a coffeehouse quick enough,
   and if the froth doesn't settle in the cup,
    I can usually remember one or two really cool lines," he replied.

"Oh," her voiced dropped. "I thought you were a poet, not just a caffeine junky."

Sometimes

Sometimes

when tension knots

frustration mounts

and routine tasks twice put-off come now to haunt;

when I just want to 'screw it all,'

find some small hole to jump in, pull the earth around me

to escape,

to be alone but not so all alone,

away from maddening chaos;

leave and not return,

wipe slates and start afresh;

when there's no one to touch,

no one for talk,

for reaching out,

no time to decompress

I want to cry but can't;

when hanging on by fingernails the twig I've grasped begins to splinter

and to snap,

it's hard not to think

something big is gonna break

or has …

and I've just missed it.

Alethea

And what's your name, young one, he asked,
    what shall I call you here?
And where're you from, he probed again,
    Intimidating, stirring fear.

Alethea, they call me here
    but few can spell my name,
and fewer still know where I'm from
    for home is far away.

And where're you bound, he wouldn't stop,
    your journey, where's it to?
Do you have plans to stay awhile
    or are you passing through?

It's not your mind to know, kind sir,
    my origin or my home.
For where I'm bound you cannot come;
    I travel there alone.

Your dress of colors bright, he mused,
    so fair a raiment nice,
delights my eye and makes me smile.
    Will you just spend the night?

Her eyes she lowered to her feet;
    her sandals he did note.
Mud covered, caked, her ankles smudged,
    her skirt she did draw tight.

What did she feel this morn right then,
    it was both fear and fright.
Alone but strong, no need to flee,
    she turned and left his sight.

Her journey's now a memory
    of colors bright and fresh,
and those she met along the way
    remember her today.

Alethea does now know herself
        as few have ever known
Her journey ended, self-complete
        she now has found her home

And home it is for meaning dear
        and hurts that long have healed;
she welcomes now a loved one old
        who from time's mists appeared.

The two of them were on a search,
        for years they ne're did meet,
but thought and heart did intersect
        to make their meeting sweet.

Surviving time and sufferings sharp;
        Old scars their mirrors show,
and by their wounds now they're made whole,
        and each of each now know.

Lonely Season

Cold dead leaves bound across
        this morning's rain-swept streets
their shattered edges battered by winds
        as fall bleeds grays and browns to winter's white

Mornings now are empty
        falling hard
as ashen chill invades oak planks and takes up
        residence in kitchen, bath, and hall

In this solitary bed I bunch into a ball
        and pull the covers tight

Remembering togetherness requires self-willed pain
        and absence so acute
so awkward that these days alone
        cannot but hanker to be filled
as if a penance has been run
        and reconciliation for past griefs not yet assuaged

Convention now keeps hearts apart
        marks space where all can see that anguished separation

Alone we move each day connected by some
        tenuous thread of memory
wisps of voice that
        tether fast two souls from long ago
to touch this heart in ways no one can see
        and brush this brow so tenderly it makes
                for tears

True Gifts

Block letters deeply etched and sharp
    into the bracelet's bar,
        with loving thought and detail
            she crafted, drew, with care.

So bright and strong and heavy
    around his wrist he'd bear
        that ensign of his lover
            whose love was pure and fair.

Two pearls he mounted in a ring,
    bright gold, pearls touching not;
        he offered these so simply set
            with love from all his heart.

The innocence of love's exchange:
    his gift too bold for words;
        his hesitation .... would she wear
            such symbol of his care?

And she, would bracelet wrap around
    his wrist for all to see
        that some unknown, unmet dear one
            from far had chosen thee?

So in the night those gifts did pass
    betwixt two hearts afar,
        and joy unbounded did leap up
            when wrappings fell to floor!

The bracelet fit sans just one link
    but Adler's mended that,
        and ring her finger did embrace.
            She'd n'ere had gift like that!

Some three fortnights now since that day
    have fled, two hearts diverged,
        but gifts so long ago bestowed
            in memory have emerged.

Such simple things, so complex yet
    when memory hearts awake;
        two lives so differently evolved
            reached out to mend the break.

A bracelet marked in memories true
    years gone but still such things,
        a little ring, two pearls no less,
            still caused two hearts to sing.

So lost is found! Her gift he wears,
    time-worn, scratched, name effaced,
        upon his heart in memory held,
            that "WILL" his wrist embraced.

That once-round circle's bended now,
    the twin pearls too are gone
        except in hearts where gifts renewed
            each time she put it on.

Could we but tell our own young sons
    to risk and not to fain.
        Those feelings, thoughts, and deepest dreams
            renew in years' return.

So let us give our memories
    into each other's care
        and dare recount our journeys true,
            new friends with friendship rare.

Madeira Tears

Tears fell from her eyes to his cheeks
    warm, wet drops of lovers' dew.

His gaze fixed her for all time
    in heart and memory.

"Why tears?" he mused.
    "I've missed you all these years
    and just now owned my loss," she whispered,
    choked through yet another tear.

And from that moment

    two hearts, new joined,
    began to beat as one.

Ambivalence

A stranger among colleagues,
    this distance so to feel,
    to walk among you daily
    and sense here life unreal.

We serve the very same God
    who in love did us make;
    but walk with me while praying,
    and you'll learn how much I've changed.

In depths of this old aging heart
    I've walked this way so steep;
    so seismic-great are changes
    that touch my soul so deep.

In solitude and silence
    I dance God's grace each day.
    I walk and pray each morning
    in gratitude and praise.

Though journeys authored long ago
    still mark my hours and days,
    familiar things seem strange now;
    they test and stretch and craze.

Here now my spirit's tested;
    this much I know for sure:
    my life, my love, my heart and soul
    have been remade, restored.

So if I seem abstracted,
    distraught by life and care,
    remember change is difficult
    unless you have been there.

My world's expanded, opened
    with new insight and new hope

   I listen to each moment,
   I dwell in immanent joy.

That world is so much larger now
   includes friends far and here;
the changes that have marked my days
   confound the ones I'm near.

I know the hurts will someday heal
   as new life springs from old
   as memories we select to tend
   release the bonds that hold.

Alone

Alone, now singular and stark,
  separated now by choice,
  emptied of closeness,
  all for granted taken.

Once in union we but now a solitary I.
  How Spartan is this place
  and void?

Not to fill too soon
  but savor quiet sacred space
  and once again to know myself
  in happiness and rage.

Yet still to yearn
  not for times passed
  but those in future's store
  to move from solitary loneliness
  to solitude alone.

What deed or word or wonder walks that line of separation?
  What gifts yet to be marveled at
  rest beyond that veil?

Navel

Nestled in her belly bowl
        both firm and yet so soft
A twist of flesh where life began
        a dimple of the past

For me to touch and taste and tongue
        On summer's afternoon
Lie close and place my hand around
        on cold dark winter's moon

So smooth the approach to this sweet spot
        So gentle curved her loins
That lovely cleft in belly fold
        So hidden from my sight
Protected, safe, and gently touched
        I'm there in dreams each night

The Source

She looked up that first morning
        from a soft-pillowed crib
                and grasped between tight-pursed lips
                        as sure as kisses that had summoned her to life

That taut pert pointed orb of joy
        where milk dripped for the taking
                and in that moment slaking both thirst
                and heart

She was right then and there for all time
        bound eternally
               to her Source

Bold

Her wounds now chevrons old
from battles lost and won

Her mind is sharp
her memory keen
her eyes with hope bright wide

Her breasts still pert and firm
rest full and maiden round

Her hips quite proud
they greet the world
with haughty tilt and gait
supported once her little ones
held close but not possessed

She knows the reason that she's here
to live and love and more
She's never lost her inner joy
retained the spring of youth

The child in her peeks through her smile
in tenderness and play
The gift she gives without regret
she'll give again today

Can You Imagine

A world without mornings
A night without stars
A child without laughter
A cat without paws

A light without burning
A boy without toys
A day without sunshine
A girl without boys

A book without pages
A flower with no seeds
A ship with no rudder
A man without needs

A love that is speechless
A poem without rhyme
A heart that's not broken
Love with enough time

A circle that's bended
A bracelet that's scratched
A memory to relive
A love with no match

A heart without wonder
An eye without fire
A passion that's ended
A life that has died

If ever you wonder
How love has been formed
Take heed and remember
Your first love, your home.

Dazzled

She dazzled him with her smile

        and finished him off with her eyes

        green and sparkling

        against raven locks

        with salt and pepper temple curls

So broad that smile

        she swallowed his spirit

        whole.

His heart clutched

        shook and missed a beat

        shuddered his whole being

A Story Poem

It was his smile
His slightly down-skewed lips
Pursed not to talk but set to whisper sweets
On that warm summer's eve
That bound her heart

Frozen fast 'cross decades now
Memories cast alone
Saddened by her losses deep
Of battered heart and separations borne

She held him there, close but untouched
Occasional memory rich
A presence in her heart and mind
An absence, youth's regret

The years of pain not without joy
A child, now two, she loves
A mother, friend, and sister true
No longer yearning love

Then from the mists of time he came
She summoned him that day
His smile intact, his heart astir
A memory clear as day

She yielded to him on that night
Her boundaries she let down
And in that moment came to him
Fresh grounded gentled home

Their twin hearts bridged both time and space
The absence disappeared
A soul-healed wound too long undressed
Did now find healing balm

Now days are full again for her
And for her love as well
Who from afar has been transformed
And knows love's grace so well

Their time together makes for tales
So tender, never shrill
New friends now gasp for air in joy
And planets now stand still

Scorched

Dark clouds presage hot storms to come.
A violence born of fear
known in the past laments of souls
withered in its heat.

A *shoah* hot, its furnace burns,
destroys both child and old,
by wrenching babes from mothers' arms
and sending strong to hell.

New tyrants vie with terrorists,
their insane rages rant,
with hi-tech drones and plagues and bombs
they torch and burn and rape.

Injustice feeds a fertile field
when hate springs up at home,
takes root and nourishes long-held fears
that justify mass death.

Who will resist this timeless scourge?
Restore a world of trust,
where patience honor, love and health
arise again from dust?

Nightwalker

Tough she is who walks the night
>forlorn on roads alone,

Her hair unkempt, her slacks unzipped
>as if at ready for her next trick.

Lipstick smeared into a snarl,
>she flashes skin below her hip.

She's here alone tonight
>for coffee and two donuts.

Bag Lady

She carries her home in a paper sack
        and walks the highway like a queen.

'Nere bows her head nor begs your time,
        she owns her self and little else
            with grace.

Such grace unsettles most she meets,
        disturbs so much they turn away.

In her eyes they recognize themselves
        and wonder, but for the road-worn shoes
        the rustled skirt and food-smeared blouse ...

might that be me alone?

Reaching

"Heel!" he shouted as
>   new wind filled the sail
>   and tipped the whole hull leeward.

"Farther out," he cried, "feel the plane."

Breeze now a wind came across port quarter
>   as fine mist turned to drenching spray.

"Ready about," he barked
>   and handed her the loosened halyard.

"Hard-a-lee," came next
>   as her world became the horizon
>   and shifted yet again.

"Out here you're free from artificial power," he mused.

"It's primal, reknitting to creation,
>   our basic links restored.
>   Water, wind, hull and sail.'

With nuanced delight
>   she'd seen but once before,
>   they came about again.

Three Words

Surprised himself that day.
        Said "I love you."
        And he meant it,
        more even now than all before.

Three words
        to redefine two worlds
        and countless lives.

Three words.
        Just three.
              No more.

Uncertain Courage

I'm new to this,
>stand awed and sometimes frightened by
>the prospect,
>not at all certain I can alone survive.

Take heart in hand,
>pour into its chambers measure
>upon measure of courage,
>assuage the fear,
>soothe the hurt,
>calm the terror.

I wear my feelings like thin gauze on my heart,
>rubbing and chaffing,
>>tearing through in tears.

I Will Not Go

You'll tire of me, she whispered.
        Tire of sameness, morning coughs and headaches.

One day you'll think, "how did this happen?"

Delight will fade with the sun at dusk.
        You'll regret and draw away.

That's my fear.
        I don't go there often
        my heart splits as I approach that space.

And space it is, a chasm
        so wide it swallows all my feelings.
        I'm numb and distant from my soul
        set wandering again, alone.

I have no hold on you, my love,
        just that, my love, and it will never wane.

What can I say to your soul, to salve a wound that will not heal?

My heart breaks new to hear your fears.

I will not leave, have now returned,
        awake,

                alive to love you fresh again across all these years tending others
                    ... as well you know.

I will not leave you, I'll not go.

Proposal

Along the water's edge
        toes dug in sand
        they walked
        and stopped

He knelt in shallow pools
        looked up
        and said....
        "I want you to marry me... I mean ... ."

And then she said, "Is that a proposal?"

"Yes!"

"Try it again," she said and smiled.

"Will you be mine? I'm yours."

"Yes," she returned,
        "Yes, yes, that's better ... Yes!"

A Body Considered

I saw myself that morning
    like for the first time
    after waking from long sleep
    there I stood

In gym locker room, on a tall mirror
    there, like bug on pin
    but clean and fresh as ever felt

I'd had that form for half-century plus two
    run it, swum it, heated it to crisp in saunas
    jogged it, steamed it, pushed its limits
    on court, track, and field

Then though it was water that's caressed my skin
    and soul on mornings early
    predawn laps with hard-bodied kids of speed

But there this morn, jay-bird naked
    I stood, relaxed
    but transfixed by what I saw

Surprised I was, and modestly pleased
    with what was there
    and what was not but had been

My body, myself – in flesh and bone
    and fat and sinew
    and I did not turn away

No baby fat or child-like chubbiness remained
    no middle aged spread
    just me and all that means

My shoulders, brown from too much sun,

still level with the earth,
        no give
        no slack, but yes,
        muscle cuts apparent
        from work and workouts, both,
        not bad I think

Biceps, never hefty but now from swimming
        seem almost lean
        elongated and firm, strong and stronger still
        not patrician arms but sturdy,
        to support both thought and projects

Veins showed but slightly blue in forearm,
        hand, and fist
        but when a fist gets rounded
        veins compete and jump to surface,
        almost feisty

Chest stands flat, again from water workouts
        and that eternal breast stroke rhythm
        thrust and pull, thrust and pull

Hard-smooth pecs belie the pull required
        firm and smooth with dust-like coat of grey
        the curly hairs of age and mileage clocked

A profile shows but slight trace this morn
        of old ventral rips below the skin
        that one day must be mended, cut and sewn
        or else presage the gut that shall not be!

No six-pack here, nor four, nor two but hint-traces
        of abdominal walls cut vertical
        to secure abs that need definition
        only work and workouts can provide.

Around the back twin buns stand tight and fit
>	Younger men take note!
>	It's in the flex that bears esteem
>	and these flexes sport no shame.

Those thighs, once oaks from soccer stout
>	now slim to swimmers' laps
>	and joggers' track
>	they're cut and every tendon shows
>	'gainst sinews taught and muscles strong,

Together taken now
>	these parts on this main frame do work
>	and smell so fresh this morn
>	to new bath and daily ablution of talc
>	and coconut shampoo.

I'm glad I'm me…..no worn out bag of bones am I
>	but gentle still of self to know not to stop,
>	but just to look -- and grin!

Before it's too soon gone and then of use to none.

Milestones

Tears shed when colleagues part
        bespeak of meanings shaped by heart;
        such joyful sadness, bittersweet,
        accompanies friends who soon depart.

Ending words are not required,
        departures soon to come;
        farewell is fine, *adieu* perhaps,
        but goodbye's not the one.

Take leave you must, and journey on,
        yet share your spirit here,
        to nourish past acquaintances,
        'cross days, months, and years.

Let memory range, profound and deep.
        You've carved a place that heals
        upon our hearts as colleagues true,
        dependable, sure, and real.

So forward now! The new day breaks,
        a new horizon far.
        We'll ne're forget your passage here.
        It's sealed upon our hearts.

A poem-gift to a graduating high school senior

Prayer-Poem for Graduation's Eve

Eternal God of time and space,
of every single human trace,
our time has flown, so quickly gone
since we came to this place.

We measure years in moments now,
centuries in but a breath;
we've reached and stretched,
new boundaries set.
Profound has been our growth.

In our best moments we have heard,
we've listened and we've sought;
and we have yearned,
with mentors near,
to learn with head and heart.

So often we have wondered,
forsaking roots of home,
and wandered far from safety
for bold we have become.

Your journey's taken life in us,
your promise now fulfilled.
Vouchedsafe to us as we began,
vouchsafe and promise still.

We count the minutes breathless
until Commencement's here.
Don't leave us yet, we're not quite there;
we're ready, but stay near.

New supplicants now of worldly care
on awesome journeys set,
but lest new confidence betray
draw near, don't leave us yet!

Now if, perchance, in arrogance
we don't know how to ask,
your presence here, we now invite:
be part of every task.

Grant us in quiet spaces
of hearts and heads and souls
that we find meaning…love…and joy
in all days new and old.

So now in greatest joy we leave
with endings sacred sighs.
Tomorrow's dawning newly calls.
In gratitude…..good bye.

Amen.

SMU Baccalaureate Prayer Spring 2007

Commencement Prayer

i thank You God for most this amazing
        day: for the leaping greenly spirits of trees and a blue true dream of sky;
        and for everything which is natural
which is infinite which is yes

                                                    e e cummings

In the spirit of this prayer-poem…. let us our hearts unite.

together assembled here we today o God, thank you
        for this questing learning
        yes serving
        inquiring inspirited
        yes community

for these who so willingly with joy shared
        earthy drudge and ecstasy of learning
        -- great thanks.

for those who care
        sufficiently and with wisdom
        to advise
        teach mentor counsel
        limit and critique
        young learners
        -- unending gratitude

yes gratitude we feel and here today express
        as generations-like-years shift
        and history walks before our very eyes.

so God listen today to hearts we pray
        fill them – us too --
        with anticipations unfettered
        of dreams great and small
        soon fulfilled
        and days too soon a memory.

*"now the ears of my ears awake and
now the eyes of my eyes are opened"*

Amen. Amen.

SMU Commencement Invocation May 2007

First Dance?

What was it first about her that turned my head?
        The swish of her pony tail?

The swirl of her skirt as she rounded the corner
        in the kitchen?

Her broad smile that spread across her whole face
        and wrapped its aura around my heart?

I'm still not certain.
        Yes, that first dance.

Moonlight Dances

Sun-bronzed shoulders brown against
      her shift of cotton white,
her breasts against my chest, so soft and full,
      hold tight don't let her go.

Don't let her slip away again when this dance ends.
      Let moonlight work its magic.
Hold her heart close to your own and
      touch the tender moonbeams of her soul.

No dream is she but flesh and real,
      so music and the dance now testify.
She's warm, so warm, beneath your touch,
      but dream she is and will appear in mind for years
          to reclaim her heart and yours.

Holy God, We Bow Before You

Holy God, we bow before you.
Touch us with your Spirit's flame.
Fill our hearts with love and wonder.
Set our minds to praise your name.

Grant that in our acts of worship,
power and truth may sprout and grow,
calling us to follow Jesus,
Son of God who makes us new.

Set your spirit in us growing,
nurtured in that fertile field,
so when time comes round to harvest
we may bear abundant yields.

Send us forth to grow and flourish
in your service to abide,
boldly offering lives that matter,
never seeking space to hide.

Ever thankful, ever grateful
for your constant love and care,
we commit our time and treasure;
and our talents we will share.

Knowing that the One you sent us
calls your people to His Way,
still abiding, ever serving
Lord, forever and today.

Hymn honoring The Reverend Tony Fernandez's retirement 2012

A Child's View ... Prescience?

I wake in the morning and look outside
    all I can see is the beauty of God.
The dew on the grass, the leaves on the tree,
    through them all God speaks to me.

    1956 Published in *Boys Life*

(An early manifestation of my later panentheistic theological orientation? No accident. No coincidence. Grace.)

www.ingramcontent.com/pod-product-compliance
Lightning Source LLC
Chambersburg PA
CBHW052124110526
44592CB00013B/1745